THE WOMAN WHO MARRIED A BEAR

MARY BURRITT CHRISTIANSEN POETRY SERIES

Hilda Raz, *Series Editor*

Mary Burritt
Christiansen
Poetry Series

The Mary Burritt Christiansen Poetry Series publishes two to four books a year that engage and give voice to the realities of living, working, and experiencing the West and the Border as places and as metaphors. The purpose of the series is to expand access to, and the audience for, quality poetry, both single volumes and anthologies, that can be used for general reading as well as in classrooms.

Also available in the University of New Mexico Press
Mary Burritt Christiansen Poetry Series:

Family Resemblances: Poems by Carrie Shipers
Self-Portrait with Spurs and Sulfur: Poems by Casey Thayer
Crossing Over: Poems by Priscilla Long
Heresies: Poems by Orlando Ricardo Menes
Report to the Department of the Interior: Poems by Diane Glancy
The Sky Is Shooting Blue Arrows: Poems by Glenna Luschei
A Selected History of Her Heart: Poems by Carole Simmons Oles
The Arranged Marriage: Poems by Jehanne Dubrow
The Goldilocks Zone by Kate Gale
Flirt by Noah Blaustein

For additional titles in the Mary Burritt Christiansen Poetry Series, please visit unmpress.com.

THE WOMAN WHO MARRIED A BEAR

POEMS

TIFFANY MIDGE

UNIVERSITY OF NEW MEXICO PRESS ❖ ALBUQUERQUE

Library of Congress Cataloging-in-Publication Data

Midge, Tiffany, 1965–
  [Poems. Selections]
  The woman who married a bear : poems / Tiffany Midge.
     pages cm. — (Mary Burritt Christiansen Poetry Series)
  ISBN 978-0-8263-5652-9 (pbk. : alk. paper) — ISBN 978-0-8263-5653-6 (electronic)
  I. Title.
  PS3613.I3628A6 2016
  811'.6—dc23

                              2015017657

Cover illustration: *Querencia* (2015), courtesy of Viva Kathleen Momaday
Designed by Lila Sanchez
Composed in Dante MT Std 11.5 / 13.5
Display type is Dante MT Std

This book is dedicated to my mother and father.

Contents

The Woman Who Married a Bear

She had a lover whose eyes were black hooks
    that pierced her heart into the darkling of his body—
then winched it out, a spent, stained prize,
    a captive of his scars, his mother's blood.

She wintered on berries and thin plums,
    relied on the mercy of trees, their crafts—
knitted traps to snare wood rats and grouse,
    while her husband groaned and slept.

She had a lover whose fingers spun viscid webs,
    who wove his nerves around her throat—
a necklace of swarm and teem, sorrow's breath,
    moth wings fluttering against her skin.

Evenings, his voice edged the cords coiled
    along her spine like a harp. His dreaming hands
arranged the dark veil of her hair, quickened into song,
    each plait a river of sound combed between his claws.

She had a lover who spooned her body at night,
    who drank from the full cups of her breasts,
who hungered for her shoulders, her mouth, her belly—
    who fed on the pounding in her chest.

The Foolish Girls

Two very foolish and lazy girls seduced an old white star, and a young red star.

They went to live with their new lovers in the star world.

—PLAINS STORY

Sister claimed the young star—chokecherry red.
When a baby she swallowed a moth and since
wanted wings. I took the white, who wheezed
when I rode him, coughed out stories from his chest—
unfathomable worlds strung like pretty beads,
all compelling yet confused. My blood's a charm
consumed by salt and the sweetest fat.
Our hearts dished out their darkest jams.
Seasons passed. I wondered. What hungers
did we avoid from the lands below?
Here, Sister wears a rag, her beauty eclipsed
by her glittering lover. Here, the stars keep
white bones stashed in a pile. While the stars
sleep, the bones rattle and teethe.

Considering *Wakantanka* #1

The last time you saw him—a week
before he drowned—he gave you
a gift: an hourglass.
It was
a decorative desk-
top embellishment with small,
blue flowers entombed in the resin.

A Song for Conjuring Shelter

She asks if you believe in the stories
the wind tells you, or if you know
how they arrive: a battery of dark birds
illuminated by the body of the world.

She wants to remember the stars most of all,
how they tumbled into the small houses of gods
and looked out over the hands of trees,
those gestures, soft shapes above the current.

Come in from the rain, come in, Sweet,
before the lightning takes you—
that embrace, all of life wanting in,
song for water, song for breath.

She can carry on, one body held together
by pins; she can draw maps and voyage
on the geography of dreams just as she can bow
humbly to her failures, offer up tobacco and bread.

And even in the coldest pocket of sky, even
in the collapse of stone, dull ache of spine,
she can hold what is already there, what has always
been there, in all the faces of the moon.

Imagining Yes

I imagine that yes is the only living thing.

—e e cummings

I want to simplify certain yeses in the world:
the military yes, the ill-gotten yes, the marital yes,
every yes really meaning no, the coy, the deceived,

the tablets of yes, the stacks of divine, the chimes of gods.
There is a catacomb of yes lying in the Crypt

of the Sepulchral Lamp; the city's last yes that ever was,
shrouded in silk handkerchiefs. Rio de Janeiro's Cristo
Redentor was toppled by excessive yeses,

now the city's weak to the black dooms of no.
I want to know the old melodies of yes. The affirmations,

proofs positive, the absolutions. Even the hymns of swallow
and finch, even the peacock offers enchantments—
the power of yes. There is a eulogy of yes

spread thick on the bread of yearning and want,
the heart quiet but wanting to shout.

What are the skeletal remains of yes?
What of the ghosts? Where do all the yeses go
after the benedictions, after the harvests? If I lie very still

will yes tremble next to me, be born, not buried,
not mourned, but hold me tightly in the dark, alive?

Night Caller

The mollusk inching toward my door,
   its body a broad wet muscle of rain and ascent,
reminds me how all things are possible,
   just as the rain foretells certainty

in a language of unquestionable voice.
   I hear the night break, the moon
toss back her hair. I hear the hum
   of contentment shuddering in the grass.

The mollusk seeks direction, drinks
   in the door's pool of light, charts
a course for warmth, its horns
   pivots of radar, exclamation points,

exquisite attachments puzzling out the smell
   of water and storms. In the last twenty-four hours
there've been slews of visitors to this porch:
   half-drowned spiders, stinkbugs, furious horseflies.

We've discarded them tenderly, others
   mercifully tended and killed, unnamed shadows,
unmarked graves, wings and songs put to rest,
   lunacies of want laid down. You turn in sleep,

then wake and tell me about tropical weddings
   and masked brides, guests who speak only
the warbled tongue of sparrows, and fall back again
   dreaming your night stories, hosting the night visits—

each with its own small creature,
   each with its own grand light.

In Praise of Our Humble Kingdom

It just so happens that the cup that longs
to be a goblet pales next to the spoon

dreaming another life as a shovel—
the spoon who thinks if only the fork didn't carp

so much he might have been a sled.
From the dim hall the mirror covets the TV—

oh, to be so valorized, so worshipped.
While from the half bath under the stairs

a sink dares to imagine a receptacle of oceans.
Solitude seems a perfect kingdom for a chair

distanced from its table, a digital clock separated
from its morning bell. What is a pair of mismatched

socks that aspire for a bouquet of wool, but settle
instead for the odd argyle out of step with its mate?

The teacups doubt their saucers' fidelity
just as the sugar bowl complains to the cream,

tries to recall how they arrived to this place.
What tokens can be offered, what assurances exchanged?

It just so happens that nothing is immune
to its own vanity. All yearn, hope, or design

for something better. Even quartz
and oak reach for their grand roles, yet in the end remain

attached, devoted. Even cotton, even porcelain,
remain proud of their humble estates.

A Love Story

The bloodstain on the towel.
After making love left.
The impression.
Of a perfectly shaped pair of cartoon lips.
The cartoon kiss a shock of crimson.
I took a photo.
It reminded you of your first time.
With Midori, your then wife.
In a love hotel rented by the hour.
Which virtually populates every corner.
Of Tokyo.
Your imprint on the sheet celebrated.
The Japanese flag.
It was a thing of beauty, you said.
Our love inspiring flawlessness, you said.
Round orb of brightness.
Or panic.
Your then wife rushed to the bath to scrub it out.

Identifying the Beast

You have listened
for those webbed shadows
casting their stitch
through the house of your body—
thin as a paper cut,
dark as a spider's eye.

What drives them from the yellow-eyed forest
into your narrow camp? What northern
charm incites them? A requiem of clapping
hands, pale and feral as ghosts?
A spectacular agency, quick as a snapped birch?
Or some harrowing wail, resounding, absolute,
dividing the ocean of your skin?

You suppose it's the scent that attracts them—
a yellow-orange flame smelling
of woodsmoke, tobacco, pine pitch,
the warm imprint of your body
rising like steam from a bed of woolens and skins,
a nest of savage beauty to them,
like the swan elegance of a woman's throat.

It is these shadows
born of mercy and blood,
fathered by legend and the peril of bones,
that climb up from the cellar's
belly, twisting the door's
gray mouth to take scraps from your table.

Irrevocably tragic
how they whine and scrape at the walls,
stalking from room
to room like your twin self gone mad,
until you are forced to make pacts
with the pack—
offering up your cleanest fear,
the fattest piece of your heart.

The Cut

Last night when you scythed through the lid
of your finger cutting endives,
when the blood plumed chrysanthemum
red and I thought of arterials and flight,
the cry of some dark bird in distress,
and when you bit hard on the rolled
dish towel and I wrapped a tourniquet of black
ribbon to staunch the flow, retrieved the wing
tip of your finger from the nest of greens,
secured it gingerly back to the wound,
the sink filling with crimson, and after
we applied the pressure gauze,
taped you up cozy as a swaddled newborn,
it occurred to me then,
giving into the rind of hysteria, in that dim
light offered from the kitchen bulbs
that spectrally clicked on and off,
it occurred to me that love is a kind of cut,
a kind of violence, a creature
of eminent precision, who knows
how fierce such blood flows, the red sash
of it running thick and deep, pouring
forth indelible as India ink, sweet and sharp,
a saint's prayer, a creature without self-regard
or reasonable expectations that cuts
to the bone and severs the distance
between two oceans, leading you toward
a radiance, a wild immersion into the throat
of some gold being you begin to recognize
as yourself, as the other—
a bloodletting, a letting go, a rescue,
something exquisitely, incandescently,
cut loose and blooming.

Considering *Wakantanka* #2

My great-aunt penned verse
    exalting the beauty of the Great Plains.

I only know her from a book of her poems
    and a newspaper article she was featured in.

She'd grown up on a homestead
    and gone blind as a child. But memory

is a primal and articulate device:
    her poems are awash in colors.

The Draw

There must be a name for it,
my sensual preoccupation
with the phlebotomist in training,
some fetish or disorder, a sanguine fixation,
because when his brown hands
(so soft) introduce their warmth to my skin,
and despite my veins mere targets
to excavate, flesh diminished to doll parts,
blood just a pool from which to draw,
an attendant science—
despite this, I am a devoted patient,
one who considers needles
a kind of love charm, instruments
of affection, because it's been years
since I've been touched,
except in this way, in a clinic's room
white as sugar, and it's been years
since anyone has drawn my blood,
eased my heart's gravity, finessed
its submission, except in this way—
his hands   (so soft)
grazing the inside of my elbow,
the tourniquet stretched taut, jaws
waking the vein, that blue pulse,
and then the pop, the sucking,
the pull, a kind of kiss, the clench
of fist, a whisk of tape and gauze
as I descend, become an opened
palace, a collision of vessel
and nerve, when hours later
the results appear: the needle's
sharp bite, its rigid tension,
the blistering afterglow
a concupiscent bruise that lingers
(so soft) for days.

Teeth in the Wrong Places

> *Coyote was ripe for adventure and wanted to visit the evil old woman*
> *he'd been warned about. She lived with her two wicked daughters and*
> *those who had slept with the handsome girls were never seen again.*

> —PONCA STORY

Sister—

Coyote's just like any man,
hungry for the dark loaves
of a woman's thighs.

You peel the skin of the tongue,
they complain it's burnt, add Tabasco.
You boil the last of the turnips,
they whine, it goes down like gallstones.

Beauty's just a bite
away from want.
I've seen Fox chew
off her own limb
for just one more taste
of freedom. Mother set
the traplines near beavers'
dens—hauled in more
than she could skin.
They moved farther
upriver next spring.

What west wind blew
those men into our house?
Who ransacked the curio
shelf, the burlap quilt and button jar?
Whose boots are these tracking
swamp rot through the kitchen?
Where's yesterday's bread,
and which dolt didn't cover the butter?

Tomorrow, I'm fixing to kill
the angel of this house.

These men that come through here—
shooting lead slugs through my green
bottles; waterlogging a season of straw;
taking liberties with my good hen.

Remember that one, those moons back,
who stepped out of the beets like a jackrabbit,
and ornery as a circle saw; that other, eyes
a sweet blue, but disposition salty as piss
and vinegar in the noonday sun.

I say, Coyote's the same as any man.

Sister—
desire's fixed to cut a tooth.
Sister—
I'm set to start grinding.

If he's still here come morning,
lay out the linen and splash
on the toilet water; put the beans
on to soak, and bring up the choke-
cherries. Lend your voice

to some pretty hymn, occupy his ears
so he's not to hear that clickety-clack
racket; that awful gnashing of teeth
going on *down there*; should he ask,
say how bitter an autumn we've had,
wouldn't he like to keep you warm?

Then fasten your eye to his fly,
give his nether regions a good scratch,
fall open to the place where the moon rides up—
North of the trapline, in a thicket of hairy frost.

Sister—
desire's fixed to cut a tooth.
Sister—
get set to start grinding.

Teton Valley

Strange to think you're my ambassador
to this wilderness. Strange to think the firearm
cinched to your hip should stall
a moose or mountain cat. Inhale,
the clouds labor like a gray lung.
Exhale, a reckoning to come.
                              Kitty says the sky's a fist—
and that rain's a liturgy heard through the skin,
easing the burden of dust and August's slow burn.
                              Strange to say I won't give in
to the empty spaces to fill, that I won't sift
through the kernels of what's been given,
and what's been received.
                              I can't keep track.
This afternoon, just before the storm
turned up, the lawn mower orphaned
in the yard, the black Lab worrying her teeth on a bone,
ears cocked for the inevitable—
I remembered to ask you: What moment
did this hard summer begin?
I can't decide just like I can't decide
about the wind. Strange.
                              Still there is this:
among the cosmos a butterfly taps her wings—
a Morse code or frequency
intended to unburden the world.

Considering *Wakantanka* #3

Since childhood,
her mother bore a scar
on the heel of her hand. Cut
from climbing her neighbor's rose
trellis. Over forty years later and miles and miles away,
her daughter meets and falls in love
with the neighbor's grandson.
These scars, roses, arrows
that bloom and bloom.

An Interior of Mythical Territory I Seek to Believe

These are the landscapes.
These are the maps.
These are the rice-paper fragilities charting
a course through what you feared
were impassable terrains.

   A list:
the cockroaches he stores in tissue
in an oak box next to his bed. Provisions
for a long journey into wilderness.
Funny, last night you secured rattle-
snake tails and displayed them like curatives,
a love medicine your Sioux cousins
warned you about. It was the Remingtons
and Colts that got you. He unloaded
the clips with iron expertise
until something beetle-iridescent glimmered
and you shook loose
in the intrepid current of his arms.

   He speaks of rivers, of aspens and firs
along those rivers, of the Tetons
that snake a path through his heart
making him weep, they spell home,
his totem place, wishbones in the pine.

   There are the longneck bottles of Coors,
offerings of tobacco, handfuls of dark earth.
There's the German grandfather he's named for,
over seven feet tall, walking home
from a day's labor, whipping and snapping
cottonmouths in two as he lurches
effortlessly over cattle and barbed wire.

There is elk viscera, denimed men
who love America, backwoods stories of cat.
The sky brews gunpowder and lightning
as two men sing outside a trailer
about sorry, brokenhearted souls and the wide-
open throat of this land.

        Would you settle for less?
Can you settle for less? Forego the shapes
of safer shadows in the trees, forego even certainty?
You guess not, because when the moon fades
out in the morning light and the sun
renders everything down to rust,
and he repeats over and again
how hungry he is for you, even your mistakes
sound like a ballad that will save you.

        And he's got you believing in the lynx,
believing that today is the longest
day of your life, believing in the hexing
properties of relics and charcoal—it's those forever-
colored eyes or that view from a summit
just outside town on the warmest night
of the year.

        It's simple then.
You've reached a plateau in a region unexplored.
And when you take your rest,
the water from the creek
tastes stronger than you imagined.

Desire: An Inventory

How is it that want begins? Or desire ends? And does it begin and end, or is it a continuing stream constantly redirected toward another target?

Is desire an origami crane folded into itself, paper wings constructed from folly? Can desire be overly delicate, overly crafted, overly *precious?*

Desire is utterly fickle. Or is it? Maybe not.

My friend, a brilliant poet, wrote a list poem in startling detail about every penis she had ever touched, and portraits of the men they were attached to. Despite my nagging she wouldn't publish it. I keep the poem interned in my file cabinet, like a prisoner or some infectious disease held in containment. Or maybe Pandora's box.

Once my want drastically plummeted after someone misspelled my name in a note. There are many ways to extinguish desire.

You think desire is a delicate impulse, but really if it had a face it would resemble a troll, or worse, a gargoyle. I only say this because desire is monstrous—the most monstrous emotion since envy, since hubris.

All rivalries can be explained by sexual conquest or sexual disappointment, by those consenting and by those triangulated, and by jealousy and fear.

Usually desire must live undetected, a shut-in within a hermitage of isolated design. Even when desire is reciprocated, we still—even then—keep it veiled beneath heavy gauze.

I have a friend who rarely reveals what she is feeling, who is always guarded. As a result, her boyfriend was always insecure—always wanted her to qualify her affection. Once, attempting to reassure him, she meant to tell him she loved him to death. Only she accidentally said, I love you *like* death.

Desire is one of those crazy, yellow moons: you can't get a purchase on its fathoms absolutely, so it's contained lest we're dragged out into the night.

Desire is seldom reasonable, even when it tries to be. It remains a petulant child and will become hysterical when persuaded. So we try to placate it, patronize it, but its will is oceanic.

"Tell me what you want," he said.
"You," she said. "I want to *want* you."

"Tell me what you want," she said.
"You," he said. "I want to *not* want you."

Trigger Warning: An Aubade

What is the perfect way to die?
How would you describe abundance
sweet as bacon fat? Darling, I'll tell you:

while keeping watch on a pan of cooking eggs,
that morning in my kitchen,
clad in boxer shorts, dangling a lit cigarette

from your lips, and clicking
the cylinder of a Colt 45,
you conjured Wyatt Earp,

the Iron Chef and Casanova.
The joke was about Mary Rowlandson
and captivity narratives,

what followed was a reenactment
of colonial lust on my red Formica table—
some lewd scene straight from the annals

of historical witness: *Pocahontas Meets John Smith;*
Sacagawea Saves Lewis and Clark;
Innocent Exotic Encounters Widowed Puritan.

While outside the sun rose like yolk—
forks and plates and a pistol set down,
redemption hooked to your rib like a burr

as I settled for nothing smaller,
because nothing but death is larger
or more grandiose than this.

Considering *Wakantanka* #4

Every March since her mother died
  the daughter's house becomes a dormitory
    for ladybugs—the mother's pet affinity. They
      emerge from the window bases, in the woodwork
        corners, and in the spokes of the heating vents. So
          instead of flowers, on the anniversary of the mother's
          death, the daughter releases a store-bought swarm
            at graveside beneath a magnolia tree in full flower.

Funeral for a Sioux Elder

Grandma Charity said *everyone wear white*
    to my funeral—perhaps the dolor color
of widows is too bleak? She won't say. Blind

at ninety-eight, we don't ask, but imagine, it's clear
    enough, her last request: she wants a door-
way opened to Heaven, wants the pure church-

goers noticed inside the Presbyterian church
    her father founded. She wants the white
man's hymns resounding loud, wants Basil Red Door,

her preacher-father, to hear it. She wants "colorless"
    devotion, for my Sioux cousins to clear
the way, for our voices to sing, oh sing, *blind*

but now I see. We went to task, blinded
    by acres of dust, years of debris in the deserted church.
We cleaned windows and beams, cleared

cobwebs and nests; walls gleamed white
    with fresh paint; the floor bleached to the color
of old bones; the pews aligned and the front doors

opened, at last. We imagined Basil Red Door
    and Grandma, and all the relatives before, blinded
by the immaculate, the spick-and-span flawless color.

Were there ghosts? The graveyard's church
    housed a faded world, line upon line of white
crosses, plastic flowers, relics anchoring the clear

open skies while the wind staked its own clearing
    beyond the living's embrace. *Think of it as a door,*
someone whispered. Funeral day, sun bore down, white-

hot, merciless, and all us cousins a blinding
    row of seeming snow. We gathered and filled the church
to bury her; respectful to her request, the only color

worn was white. Yet what's a day without *some* color,
    some flaw? Ex-wife's baby in tow, Jamie Clear
Fast arrived, all whirlwind, all chaos. The church

walls seemed to buck in protest as the doors
    swung open; the men, jolted into a blind
rage, Geronimo mode, jerked Jamie out to his white

pickup, blindsided him from every angle—clearly
    he'd earned it. Blood colored the lot, the church
looked on, even Charity, even Basil Red Door, all in white.

Distress

The waiter refills my glass,
then a crash
almost collapses the awning
outside. Rain staccatos the roof.
I think of bullets.
                    Earlier on the phone
when you gave the details,
it seemed a murder took place.
But it hadn't; rather your brother-in-law
and his mother had both suddenly
died within their heat-soaked
and asphyxiated house, amid
rooms and rooms and rooms of books.
"Natural causes," the police told you,
heart panics, heat strokes of sorts,
and I wondered how such deaths
could possibly be "natural."
                    In Kosovo, little boys
ran after your interpreter's
VW Rabbit begging for cigarettes. What is a Newark
house with too many books?
What is a torn country? *They love Americans!*
Because we bombed the Kurds.
                    It pours outside.
The sky's a fist of tobacco,
and the night smells like pennies and blood,
our first rain in months.
From my current read, *The Bookseller of Kabul,*
I tell you that the Taliban outlawed
kite flying but not polygamy.
                    My windshield wiper breaks.
I drive home with your bath towel
in my lap, Scotch tape holding
the blade together. You fly back East
to see to burials and labyrinths of books,

unforeseen rain that surrenders
to gravity, a luminous source of light
trailing from war-torn cities.

The Boy with No Eyes

the boy with no eyes
arrives out of dust   oily rags   rust
his twisted face appears in rearview mirrors
when you are driving
                              highwaylonelyatnight
he arrives
out of the hiss and spit of tires on blacktop
from cold damp clouds winched from the missouri
from broke necks   cracked spines
and gossips milled from small border towns like this
he arrives from your perfect and intimate sins
the fretwork of a dark passenger's face
he arrives
                              and departs
between the sky's gray cloth
and every white cross you see
staked roadside

Soothe

Their mother, schizophrenic, loathes
the color red: fire trucks, stop signs, cuts.
Red conveys treachery, discord,
sex. Anything brownish is also a threat—
too reminiscent of filth or decay,
a color deserving of contempt and scrubbing out.
Of all colors, white is safe:
bedsheets, lilies, nurse uniforms.
All of their house furnishings
gleam white, reliable as returning
geese: white chairs, white couch,
white rugs. Meanwhile, her children,
ill at ease, orbit pristine chambers precisely,
so carefully, little potential stains
of doom, sweet bullets. However,
the wintery months redeem them:
snow cottons atop branches, tinsels
amid streets and rooftops, cradles lawns, bushes
like fog, like smoke, white feather boas
shaken from clouds. Relief.
As if removing a corset, drawing that first breath
of cold, brisk air. Their mother slips
calm the color of doves over her thin shoulders,
smooths her ease over hip bones
like some loose gauze of silk. A leisured lady's stocking.
The chaos stills, her mind a snow globe's blizzard
at rest. Their mother anew,
like a babe soothed by milk,
wandering into the drift.

Mayflower

Someone said Nez Perce country reminds her of Tuscany
or Umbria and today on my drive through these yellow hills
I might just agree except for the Mayflower truck
straining its sails against the impossibly steep grade
banked by the metal figures of Sacajawea and good old
Lewis and Clark. Last month coming off this same grade
I was pulled over for speeding and when the cop asked
where was I going I regret not telling him
to the rez to pick up drugs
even though that's exactly what I was doing.
I've been reading articles by an Indian writer
who is accused by another Indian writer
of not comprehending irony. My drives to the Lapwai
clinic for my monthly pickup give me time
to think about these things. I've always thought
irony is instilled by birthright when you're Indian
and if it's missing something might be seriously wrong
with you. These same hills remind me of the wooly
backs of animals—horses I guess like the Appaloosas
the Nez Perce are stewarding. Today I have a different
kind of Appaloosa that's slow to the grade
and I must have climbed up this hill about a thousand times
in every direction.

Considering *Wakantanka* #5

your close friend   maynard   while walking on a highway
at night is struck by a car and loses both his legs   he lives
the same week it happens   you are reading an old anthology of poetry
in it   a poem titled   *to maynard on the long walk home*
about a bicyclist killed   in a hit and run

Antiquing with Indians

First it was the tumblers for highballs—
cocktail hour with primitives,
the kind your grandma wore her red dress for.

Thirty dollars seemed too steep, even for a stereotype,
even for bones, perfect and white, snapped through
afros, pierced through noses, prehistoric as flint.

Still you wanted them, even if you don't drink
anymore. Then it was the Battle of Little Bighorn
board game, replete with war-bonneted Sioux

and Cheyenne, action figures on horseback;
plastic Gatling guns and cannons,
tomahawks and war shields galore.

But you're above all that. Except for the beaded Indian
doll, the pincushion with a wrist clasp—
you want to be that Indian wearing the Indian

like a Russian doll, you want to uncover
and uncover, go undercover and pin yourself
back to completion again; buy the beaded skirt

for those days when voodoo seems a viable option
(you know the ones). The moment we entered the store,
the real life version

of Pocahontas and John Smith,
a voice from the back called out, *squaw man* . . .
Later we found the 1906 novel the voice was referring to.

Don't you want to be more than a metaphor?
That's the beauty of it, that's the trick;
you think ironies are free, but they're not.

Latona mentioned how she'd discovered
a Tonto doll, stoic and monosyllabic,
seated next to a Custer puppet,

which had so unnerved her she felt it her duty
to relocate Tonto to a more auspicious corner—
someplace safe next to doilies or Fiestaware.

What wars might emerge from such proximity?
she'd wondered. What skirmishes could result?
I imagined the Iroquois brave

brandished on the alfalfa-seed cloth sack
could overtake the Yakama squaw apple box,
succeed his throne beyond the Calumet baking powder's

proud profile. *Don't mess with vintage,*
the collections seemed to warn. *If you think
this is* Toy Story, *you got another thing coming.*

Code Name *Geronimo*

In 2011 someone made an order, kill *Geronimo*.
Soldiers dispatched by jet, by jeep, orders to kill a.k.a. *Geronimo*.

The Brits had a new princess and Fergie's daughters wore silly hats,
but the royal wedding was eclipsed by the killing of a.k.a. *Geronimo*.

I heard about it on the radio, bin Laden's been ratted out
living in a pleasant Pakistani suburb, *KIA Geronimo*.

He used his wives as shields, there is nothing about
that fact to cheer yet some did after killing a.k.a. *Geronimo*.

For tribal nations the namesake's a hero, little doubt
occupies their minds as to the military's code *KIA Geronimo*.

It's just another cry for war without
restraint. Our hero wasn't a terrorist, the *real* Geronimo

fought to protect homelands, way of life, I'd say devout,
and feared. Tell me, how many times should they *kill* Geronimo?

(Dis)beliefs Suspended

There is a Winnebago story about Coyote. In order to win the heart of the chief's handsome son—in order to win status and power—Coyote seduced the son by pretending to be a beautiful young woman. On their wedding night Coyote fashioned a faux vagina from the liver of an elk. It was all believed, so much so that Coyote actually bore the Chief's son several fine, strong children.

The verisimilitude, it's all there. The breathtaking scenery—you know they're just facades and painted backdrops, but you dream them into reality anyway. You believe in them because if you don't believe, what is left? If the canyon is a fresco wash ablaze with stunning pinks and mauves, a canvas that both dazzles and compels you into believing that you are touching fates and magic, and even though you know it's half false, half trickery, you reach out for it anyway. It is so intimate and so finely mastered—you *have* to touch it. You have to pull it into your body like a drink of water that will save you. And you're assured that it will, that it already has. You know about the feral nature of such illusions, and you realize the hazards.

Who becomes more the fool? The one who believes or the one expert in casting illusions? Even the one who dispels trickery believes. Perhaps they believe the hardest of all. Coyote is a catalyst. And all catalysts, whatever their bag of tricks, can and will save you.

Considering *Wakantanka* #6

A man whom she desperately,
without dignity or reason, desired,
kept his heart fixed to an old lover.
One day, provoked by jealousy,
she spoke his old lover's name
and wished her dead.
A little more than a year later,
the old lover is consumed with tumors
leaving two young children
and a husband to mourn her.

Abstraction

I awoke this morning missing my heart. It was wrenched from my chest and taken into custody by the fur trapper from Iron Horse Lake. I'm told he collects them like cut pelts—trophies from the wilderness—and exhibits them next to the oak and inlaid-ivory gun rack hanging over his bed. I'm told he has quite the collection, each with distinguishing properties and carefully labeled signatures. Mine reads: 1965, Sioux Girl with Pearl Scalp. The others are not so plain. He spends weeks sharpening his knives against the tenderness of their nerves, honing his craft for the thrill of pursuit, sharpening his sense of smell, encroaching their territories, rooting out those damp caves where his souvenirs sleep. I'm told when the hearts are gathered and each chamber bled out and exposed, he makes a portrait of them, an installation for the throngs of curious eyes—those hungry patrons of the arts, who marvel at the dark, elusive canvases of the absurd.

After Viewing the Holocaust Museum's Room of Shoes and a Gallery of Plains' Indian Moccasins: Washington, DC

The portrait is clear:
one is art
the other evidence.
One is artifact
the other atrocity.

Each is interned
behind glass,
with diagrams
and panels,
a testament to miles
walked. Both
are worn,
each a pair,
one is cobbled,
one is beaded.

At my tour's end
can I buy a key-chain shoe?
Will I be assigned
the ID card
of one of the perished
at Wounded Knee?

The moccasins
are beautiful. Seed pearls
woven intricate as lace.
We don't mourn
the elegant doe skins,
we admire the handicraft.
We don't ask whose soles
these relics come from.
We don't look for signs of resistance,
or evidence of blood.

Nor do we wonder
if he was old
and passed in his sleep,
or if this child
traded for a stick of candy
or a pinch of dried meat.
We do not make assumptions
of original ownership at all.

Their deaths were not curated,
not part of an installation. We
don't absorb their violent
or harrowing ends under soft
lights or dramatic shadows.

We look right through them,
more invisible than the sighs
of ghosts.
And then we move
on to the next viewing,
and the next,
and the next,
to another
collector's trophy
lying
beneath a
veil of glass.

Considering *Wakantanka* #7

The couple drove along the roads of southern Oregon, through the logging terrains and byways, when they heard about the death of Ken Kesey on the radio. In those precise moments a rock—which they imagined must have been dropped from above by a passing bird—struck the windshield. And in the next microsecond of the next microseconds, they whizzed past a white-haired man traveling with a walking stick on the side of the highway.

A Postcolonial Irony

Picture it: A cold Monday evening at a coffee shop.
Leah and I poring over postcolonial texts
for our postcolonial course, highlighting "imperialism"
and "white privilege" and "supremacy" in lime green—
reconciling terms by Fanon and Said and hooks
in a neon pink that paints the words as astonished bystanders,
when the door whisks open, an impatient yawn,
wintery-brisk air spills into the room, a rez woman
clad in an oversized T-shirt and flip-flops, a face mapped
with years of nicotine and drink, a face
intimate with a hunger we've never known,
would never know, of a postcolonial legacy.

She poised at the entrance, tentative, as if thinking
she didn't belong; taking in the view of us, our important
books, our important laptops, our taken-for-granted
comforts. Understand, Leah is blonde and pretty
as an L. L. Bean catalog model,
I am of undeterminable ethnicity, white and Lakota
and mostly passing. The woman addressed
us, her posture both comic and cavalier—

"Are there any bars around here?"

And without missing a beat,
but obviously missing everything else,
we pointed her in the direction of the Alley,
the Garden, while she cradled her bare elbows against
the frigid air, waited with resigned patience,
while we courteously and with nice, *white*-girl smiles
plotted her course toward destruction,
reinforcing the instruction of her ruin.

It happened so quickly,

I didn't even think

to call her *Sister*, to invite her in from the cold,
offer her a cup of coffee instead.
The rez woman thanked us and returned
to the dark street, whatever her next destination,
for that something warm to slide down her throat,
to both ease and stir the fire inside her chest,
to warm her heart and nurse the survivor/warrior wound—

a bottle of something big enough
to make all of us forget.

What Is the Sound of America?

Did Chief Joseph hear the Dixieland jazz,
the ragtime jubilees and house parties,
the evangelist bands playing Pentecostal hymns
on hot, summer nights? Was he there
for the doo-wop, the creek river rallies,

the syncopation, that grind and gyration
of hips and spines on a hardwood floor?
Did he hear, *Wow the crowd,* on a quarter acre
of heartbreak? Did Chief Joseph ask:
Are you a musician or an entertainer?

Their hymnals transposed to bell and drum,
from the old ledgers, from the King James Bible.
And did he speak the language of the later gods?
Dizzy Gillespie, Coltrane, Miles Davis,
Louis Armstrong, Duke Ellington, Cab
Calloway, and Charlie "Bird" Parker?

This is what happened when the missionaries
tried to convert our heathen souls:
the Lollipop Six, Nez Percians, Jack Teagarden,
International Sweethearts of Rhythm,
Scrapper Blackwell, "Big Chief" Russell Moore,

Dan Beyhylle and the Ten Little Indians,
Junior Walker and the All Stars, Buck
Clayton, Pee Wee Russell, Harry "Fox" McCormick,
Chief Shunatona and the All Indian Band.
What is the sound of America?

The *ching-chinga-ching, ching-chinga-ching*
of brush strokes against a brass cymbal?
A 49er, *I don't care if you're married*
I'll get you yet, I'll take you home in my one-eyed Ford?
Horns so anguished they made people weep?

Buglers dodging flying bullets?
Survivance. This is the sound of survivance.
The sound of wind whistling through the Snake River Canyon.
The sound of a stomp dance, bells and seeds.
The sound of "Indians Playing the White Man's Jazz."

Spring Valley Reservoir

Some things are necessary, the pheasant
for instance, her call claimed first in the chest,
an elegant not wholly unpleasant
thrum as if a small being has made a nest
below your ribs, then strikes her way out.
Or the heron who wreathes the water
dragging along a veil of mist like white-
lace meteors along the reservoir
banks. We need the osprey, her acrobatic
plummets for bluegill, her aerial craft,
the way we need air, water, light. The creek
runoff pitches into a green prayer mat
of marsh amazed by its own silk body.
We live on this: the wings, the rhapsody.

Her Kind of Horses

—After Laura Tohe & Joy Harjo

Yesterday, I met a Navajo woman with turquoise horses. She told me there are rainbow horses, abalone horses, amethyst horses. I wondered what kind of horse carries me through this illusionary labyrinth. I live in Lapwai country, which means Land of Butterflies in the Nez Perce language, so I would guess I am carried by butterfly horses.

Yesterday, I met an Assiniboine woman named Papillon, French for Butterfly. She had a tattoo of a butterfly inked on her hand. She is one of seven daughters who was raised by a rancher. She spent all her Montana summer days as a girl breaking horses, bucking hay, mending fence. I forgot to ask what kind of horse carries her spirit, but I imagine it would be a butterfly horse also.

Yesterday, I met an Apache woman who believes in storms. She has pulled four children from her body like flowers. I wondered if her son Hawk was born or conceived during a storm. I wondered if the storm was male or female. I wondered what stone or winged horses drove her spirit, because she is soft as female rain in the mesas of this glittering world. But her heart is fierce and devoted as the hardest lightning in her loving. She is a hundred kinds of rain, a hundred kinds of storm, a hundred kinds of radiant horses.

The Night Horse

And so we say
love is the oddest moonlight
that exists. We say
the stars speak in brilliant
and shimmering tongues.
We say the night
is the only sense
there is
because only in darkness
can we begin to see.
And so we say
love is a delivery
from something called fear (that
terror like entering
the throats of wounded animals).
Remember those long ago
nights when hours of dreaming
were piercing needles to the skin,
and mouths searching to taste
the bitter salt of desire?
Those nights waiting
for the dark flash of motion
to repeat our names
in a language we feared to speak?
And so we say
love is the shape of an animal,
stepping through darkness
with the precision of knives,
arriving to this world
still moist from another.
And so we say
love is the delivery
on the backside of that night
horse. We say fear
transcends beyond
living in the dark,

night and day,
darkness and light
exchange elegant gestures
like dreams captured in a net
of frozen stars.
    And we say
    only in the dark
    do we begin to see.

For the Lummi Girl Who Found Her Magic in Horses

Every other word she spoke a sonorous *horse this,*
horse that, with an otherworldly grin that conjured
afternoons riding beneath the falling sun.

She could have been a silhouette traveling along the crimson
body of Arizona rock, or circling the backbones
of desert cliffs she'd only visited in picture books.

If she told me her horse had wings and took her on nightly flights
through the shimmering stars straight to the moon, I would have believed her.

If she told me her horse was a blazing ribbon of flame galloping
across the Pacific Ocean like a Jesus pony trotting on water,
running forever to save us, I would have believed her.

I could see she found her magic in horses.
I could see each time the word *horse* escaped from her throat,
an eruption of stretched sinew and bones of an animal too holy
to appear in daylight reached out to capture a fringe of this world's curtain.

She attempted to keep their tossing heads in the corral of her heart,
their unrestrained tricks secured beneath the fence of her rib cage,
only they continued to fly out like the laughing wild spirits they were.

Horse spirit and horse magic ignited by the dreaming of a Lummi girl
who sang their names in the shadow of sundown.
Who offered them the sweets of her voice in ragged meadows,
who called them her own in the pale blue mornings across the land she calls
    home.

One by one they leapt into the classroom air,
and she pulled hard on their reins,
led them back in.

Considering *Wakantanka* #8

My grandparent's old Deluxe
on standby in their kitchen—
the way it moaned and strained
against the steam and pressure
of the automatic drip,
the way it sounded
remarkably and amazingly human,
the way my grandfather lay dying,
how my grandmother cared for him
all hours of the day and night,
the way she kept the coffee maker
going, fresh doses all throughout those days
and nights, how it moaned and agonized,
exactly like my grandfather
as he busied himself
with the serious labor of dying.

Hinhan

In the months before her lungs flowered,
before her heart wore out,
an old enemy or a love-sick ghost
posed for days on the back patio.
My mother is superstitious and prone to worry,
a Sioux woman is taught owls
are harbingers of death.
                          She admitted once
that if she died
she'd come back a small bird—
a finch or sparrow—because she preferred
the plain and uncomplicated, the most humble,
or maybe she was trying to tell me,
reassure me, that she'd never
visit me in owl form, that creature
portending omen, theft, transcendence.

                          My mother believed
her relatives resided within the air,
breathing alongside the living—
emptying themselves as shadow
into her rose beds, her foxglove,
just as I believe that in her way
she brings forth the turn of each new season,
the rain, its starts and little deaths—

and owls, wide-eyed patrols,
constant guards in the trees.

Hinhan means young owl in Lakota.

Planting Tulips the First Autumn after Your Death

I didn't know the song for conjuring spring
or how to apologize
for every small harvest I missed.
I didn't know how to draw your name from the clouds
or unlatch the door to a new season.
It might be true
that what we lack is offered back by our longing.
It might be reclaimed
by the sound of rain, fistfuls
of hard shells clamoring to earth,
kneeling to every god
whose only design is to split us wide open
by the shapes of loss.

I didn't know how to observe autumn
or listen for your voice in the slow fade-out of the stars.
I imagined your passing differently. Your breath
caught on the unbroken surface of water,
your story collected from the salt of a lover's skin,
the ache of you resting in my palm as I sleep.

Never mind all that. In the end
I plotted tulips in a garden box
big enough to die ten times in.

For each puncture I repeated your name like a psalm.
In the end a hundred consecrations,
each their own color and lovely anticipations.

A hundred times your name,
a hundred times your breath,
a hundred times your song,
a hundred earthly chances
to ripen, to bloom.

Considering *Wakantanka* #9

After the ventilator was finally removed, after
we held our collective breath, waited for the
monitors—heartbeat, respiration—to wind
slowly down, then stop, I made my good-byes,
then left. On the way out of the hospital, a
three-year-old girl refused to let me pass until I
acknowledged her ecstatic declaration:
We. Just. Had. A. Baby!

Scenes from a Naturalist's Sketchbook

In the days following my mother's death
my father tells me the stars don't exist:
These burned out years ago,
these are what remain,
tricks of the eye.
Beneath a congress of firs
lit by those passing stars, he contradicts:
Everything still exists, it's all still alive.
I think of the intrepid current of a Cascades
creek that nearly drowned me—
the rapids I was saved from banked by stones
each with a name my father knew: *Terrigenous,*
breccias, shale. In the Gulf of Mexico
kerchiefed women, aunties of Jorge and Jose,
peddled giant sea-turtle shells to tourists—
my father shrugging them off: *Gracious, gracious, no, no.*
I think of remote camps, my father leaving
for hours on expedition, returning with a hat
full of berries he swore he'd outrun a bear for.
Nong Nooch Tropical Garden, Thailand: My father
chain-smoking Chinese cigarettes beneath
an umbrella of palms, the esplanade full of howler
monkeys and sun bears, an exhibit of giant butterflies.
Everything still exists, it's all still alive.
We net smelt at a Pacific coast beach,
fingers and hands stained purple from gutting fish,
faces stinging from salt spray, canvas Keds
drying in a row on a line; tacky residue of campfire
fish on our hands, the meat part smoke, part sweet.

Famine

Gone, the quiet of midnights past. My father boiled onions whole—
speared from fork to mouth with butter, salt.

Another midnight: pale light crowned his bald head, a moon.
Before him, a cereal bowl with Dog Chow, milk.

In Pattaya, he brought me a pot of rice after a two-day fast, reasoned
it was the utensils that made me sick, not the mango.

I pretended to want the crisp and blackened centipedes, to gnaw
through bags of crickets, find the green pearls inside.

The peasant-shack cook assured me the meat was pork. My father
laughed when I pointed to the dog beneath the table:

Tomorrow's lunch. I tried to remember a time before Dauk served
us chili and Cokes beneath a canopy of limes

and eucalyptus trees; a time before the howler monkey played chase
with a giant moth. Gone.

In the airport taxi, my head rested on my father's shoulder
the last time. I slept.

Whatcom Creek

It's been four years since I've seen my father,
and here we are taking in the mayhem
like a couple of tourists who'll later
buy bright, glossy postcards of the salmon
belly-up and gutted along the pier.
He's still handsome, my father, still smokes
the filterless cigarettes, year by year
their tar flowering like badly timed jokes
in his dark lungs. I used to pray for him
before prayer was as futile as these fish
pitching their fruiting bodies into dim,
bleary tombs. This same time next year I'll wish
for more time. I'll wish for redemption,
but only ghosts will rise, I imagine.

Considering _Wakantanka_ #10

The day I was born
my father chose my name
from a _Time_ magazine in the hospital
waiting room. My namesake was a daredevil
woman who, outfitted in parachutes recycled from old silks,
flung herself from the wings of airplanes into the mouths of rain
forests.

Acknowledgments

Grateful acknowledgments to the editors of the following periodicals, publications, and anthologies in which these poems, excerpts of poems, and poems published under different titles first appeared:

Periodicals

As Us: "Desire: An Inventory" and *"Hinhan"*
Codex: "Distress" and "A Love Story"
Cold Mountain Review: "After Viewing the Holocaust Museum's Room of Shoes and a Gallery of Plains' Indian Moccasins: Washington, DC"
Connotation Press: "The Foolish Girls"
Drunken Boat: "Night Caller," "Scenes from a Naturalist's Sketchbook," "Famine," and "Whatcom Creek"
Florida Review: "Considering *Wakantanka*," #1–10, appeared as "Ten Ways to Consider the Holy Spirit"
North American Review: "A Postcolonial Irony" and "(Dis)beliefs Suspended"
No Tell Motel: "In Praise of Our Humble Kingdom" and "The Draw"
Oregon Literary Review: "Planting Tulips the First Autumn after Your Death," "Trigger Warning: An Aubade," "Some Interior of Mythical Territory I Seek to Believe," and "The Cut"
Poetry Northwest: "The Woman Who Married a Bear"
The Raven Chronicles: "For the Lummi Girl Who Found Her Magic in Horses" and "Identifying the Beast"
Shenandoah: "Teeth in the Wrong Places"
South Dakota Review: "Soothe," "Teton Valley," "Antiquing with Indians," and "Funeral for a Sioux Elder"
Stirring: "The Woman Who Married a Bear" and "Teeth in the Wrong Places"
Toe Good: "The Boy with No Eyes"
Yellow Medicine Review: "Spring Valley Reservoir," "Mayflower," "Code Name *Geronimo*"

Anthologies

"Abstraction" appeared in *Ahani: Indigenous American Poetry,* ed. Allison Adelle Hedge Coke (Corvallis: Oregon State University, 2006).
"What Is the Sound of America" and "Her Kind of Horses" appeared in *America! What's My Name?*, ed. Frank X. Walker (Nicholasville, KY: Wind Publications, 2007).

"Abstraction," "Trigger Warning: An Aubade," "Funeral for a Sioux Elder," and "A Song for Conjuring Shelter" appeared in *En esa roja nacion de sangre: Poesia indigena estadounidense contemporánea*, ed. Victor Rodríguez Nuñez and Katherine Hedeen (Mexico, DF: La Cabra Ediciones, 2011).

"After Viewing the Holocaust Museum's Room of Shoes and a Gallery of Plains' Indian Moccasins: Washington, DC" appeared in *I Go to the Ruined Place: Contemporary Poems in Defense of Global Human Rights*, ed. Melissa Kwasny and Mandy Smoker (Sandpoint, ID: Lost Horse Press, 2009).

"Imagining Yes" and "A Song for Conjuring Shelter" appeared in *I Was Indian*, ed. Susan Deer Cloud (Kanona, NY: Foothills Publishing, 2009).

"After Viewing the Holocaust Museum's Room of Shoes and a Gallery of Plains' Indian Moccasins: Washington, DC" appeared in *New Poets of the American West*, ed. Lowell Jaeger (Kalispell, MT: Many Voices Press, 2010).

"Identifying the Beast" appeared in *Nobody's Orphan Child* (Seattle, WA: Seattle Wood Works Press, 1996).

"For the Lummi Girl Who Found Her Magic in Horses" appeared in *A Shade of Spring: An Anthology of New Native Writers*, ed. Michael Paul-Martin (Toronto: 7th Generation Books, 1998).

"Abstraction" appeared in *Sing: Poetry from the Indigenous Americas*, ed. Allison Adelle Hedge Coke (Tucson: University of Arizona Press, 2011).

"The Night Horse," "Promises of Winter," and "The Woman Who Married a Bear" appeared in *Without Reservation: Indigenous Erotica*, ed. Kateri Akiwenzie-Damm (Ontario: Kegedonce Press, 1993).

Some of these poems appeared in the limited edition chapbook *Guiding the Stars to Their Campfires, Driving the Salmon to Their Beds* (Fayetteville, AR: Gazoobi Tales Publishing, 2005).

Many thanks for the nurturance and support of my teachers, mentors, and fellow students at the University of Idaho's Graduate Creative Writing Program. Gratitude to Julie Wing and Jay Dearien: your love and encouragement have been incalculable. Special acknowledgment to Janet McAdams, Kenyon College, and the selecting committee for the Kenyon Review Earthworks Prize for Indigenous Poetry.